Wear **YES** on Your Heart

&

you can do anything!

*Wear YES on Your Heart & You Can Do Anything!*

ISBN-10 0615495427

ISBN-13 9780615495422

# Wear YES on Your Heart

## & you can do anything!

**INTRINSIC BOOKS**

Orlando, FL.

*"I cannot be an optimist but I am a prisoner of hope."*

— **Cornel West**

# INSPIRATION

*"And we know that God causes everything to work*
*together for the good of those who love God and are called*
*according to his purpose for them."*

**ROMANS 8:28 KJV**

When I was very young, just a short time after I learned of my adoption, my grandmother showed me a picture of myself as a newborn. It was an image I'll never forget, because that baby (me) was undeniably unattractive. I tell you no lie—that picture was so bad that until then it had been hidden, and I've not seen it again to this day, nor do I have any desire to. My head was shaped funny, my eyes were puffy, and my lips were as large as they could possibly be and still fit on my face. My grandmother laughed as she remembered that my toes were curled up like those of a turtle. She told me that the first time my father saw me, he looked at my mother and asked, "Are you sure about this?" My grandmother and I both laughed about that one.

However, as the laughter subsided and she put the picture away, I thought more deeply about that image. It was probably taken only moments after leaving the arms of my biological mother. I was born with a heart murmur and what appeared to be other physical deficiencies. By the time I saw that picture I had already grown numb to the sting of poverty, acquainted with the streets, bound to working the oppressively hot produce fields of Florida, bankrupt of self-esteem, and deprived of a good education. I realized then, that for me there would be little given, and worse, even less expected. For a time, I even bought into everything that suggested I could amount to little more than nothing. Throughout my teenage years things only grew worse, but the difference between that bankrupt kid and the man who went on to be successful in the military, a scholar in college, a mentor to youth, and the type of person who makes a habit out of making his dreams come true, was one simple thing—Inspiration.

I found inspiration in being given up for adoption and in the love of my adoptive parents, who never—not once—made me feel as though I was anything less than of their own making. I found inspiration in wanting to be someone whom my six younger siblings could look up to and my parents could feel proud of. I found inspiration in my determination to prove wrong the people who said I couldn't be anything, who laughed at my ambitions, and who tore me down every chance they had. I gained inspiration from the teachers and counselors who believed I could do more and, ironically, I drew more from the principal who told me to my face I would never amount to much, and that I may as well catch an early start on quitting. I even found inspiration in the thought of being carried for nine months by a woman who knew she was going to give me away. From the moment she found out she was pregnant to the moment the nurse walked out of the barren hospital room with her child, I can only imagine what she had to go through, mentally, physically, and emotionally. She had enough love to go through all of that anguish and pain just to give me a chance at life. Her love inspires me. From the sprouting of a flower through the earth to the most powerful life changing circumstances that we may experience in our lives, I realized that inspiration could be found in and drawn from anything, if we only allow ourselves to see it.

I value inspiration and the opportunity to inspire people because I am a living testimony of what it can do. Wear YES on your heart and you can do anything. I've been told the sound of that ranges from corny to cliché, but I couldn't care less, because I wholeheartedly believe that when we choose to wear YES on our hearts rather than doubt, worry, the feeling of being undeserving, and the attitude of "I can't", there is nothing that we cannot do.

In the event that our motivation runs dry, we should all have a well of inspiration to draw from. My well is the story of an Israeli man named Ami Ankilewitz, diagnosed with a rare disease at birth, a disease that limited his growth to only 39 pounds at the age of 34, and his physical movement to a single finger on his left hand. Yes, he was born with a devastating disease, but he was also born with dreams and a burning passion in his heart. His dreams were to become an animator and to one day see America. Despite overwhelming odds, this man has lived 30 years beyond everyone's expectations, has journeyed to America, and is today a successful animator.

Can you even begin to imagine or comprehend what life would be like to be an adult the size of a small child with the ability to move only one finger? The vast majority of us are able-bodied and of sound mind, yet we allow ourselves to be talked out of believing in ourselves by those around us, our circumstances, and sometimes by our self-destructive thinking.

Ami Ankilewitz dared to dream, and the passion of his heart made those dreams a reality. His story, among many others that we are blessed to witness and hear about, is proof that when you wear YES on your heart, you can do absolutely anything. Inspire, allow yourself to be open to inspiration, and be prepared to inspire yourself, because sometimes you will feel that you have no one to depend on but you. Just make sure that inspiration lives in your life, so that you can truly bring the most out of it.

If today was tough, speak a better tomorrow into existence.

———————

There is strength in vulnerability, power in the act forgiveness,
and peace in the midst of your every storm.

———————

The best way to predict the future is to create it!

———————

You can grin at your failures when you know they will only make
your successes that much sweeter.

———————

Don't let the fear of failure turn you into the coward that
that only saw their dreams.

Don't run away from the problem, it only creates distance from the solution.

———————◆◆◆———————

A strong person can pretend all is well when it's not, a stronger person can admit they are going through, and ask for help.

———————◆◆◆———————

Only you can stand between you and what God has for you.

———————◆◆◆———————

Success comes with the realization that you can make more opportunities than you will ever stumble across.

———————◆◆◆———————

Sometimes you have to believe what you feel, even when no one else sees the sense of it.

The first step of achieving growth in strength is identifying
the root of your weaknesses.

---

It doesn't matter your circumstance, God can.

---

You don't have to be sure about what your future holds
when it's being held in God's hands.

---

At times the journey may seem daunting, but only God knows
how far we have to run when chasing our dreams.

---

Be aware of your limits, but never afraid
to attempt exceeding them.

Don't let obstacles deter you
to a clear path with a lesser goal.

———————————◆—◆—◆———————————

Today's troubles are tomorrow's testimonies.

———————————◆—◆—◆———————————

Just as joy continues to be rediscovered in rain, there is always
production that may be found in pain.

———————————◆—◆—◆———————————

The beautiful thing about the future is we don't have to wait until
a New Year or birthday, it starts right NOW.

———————————◆—◆—◆———————————

It's better to make risks to be happy,
than to be certain in misery.

For as much as you may have to sacrifice for success,
you better not give up on the path to it.

———◆———

Don't ask God "why me", someday your pain is going
to be useful to you and a blessing to someone else.

———◆———

You were born with the green light to
GO for your dreams.

———◆———

Everyone has a story, and the ability to make
the next person's a little better.

———◆———

Be defiant!
Come at life twice as hard.

The sky isn't high enough for you, keep reaching.

---

No use in fearing death. You may as well live your life so you can have something to smile about on the way out.

---

The thing about life is nobody gets out alive, so you may as well live!

---

You may not have made the right choice,
but you can always make the right change.

---

Sometimes the only obstacle standing between you
and happiness is YOU.

You don't look back when walking with God because what's in front of you is GREATER than what is behind you.

---

Fall doesn't have to mean fail; we learn to win when we lose.

---

When someone tells you what you can't do, turn it into the fuel you need to do the "impossible".

---

Despite it all, sometimes you just have to hold your head high and keep moving forward.

---

You can have the passion and belief, but you need ACTION as well to make your dreams come true.

If you are going to regret the past and worry about the future, the very *least* you can do is make the best of today.

———◆◇◆———

Life is an ongoing lesson, good day or bad, just be grateful you are still in the class!

———◆◇◆———

There isn't a moment that isn't a miracle.

———◆◇◆———

Failure is guaranteed when you give up.

———◆◇◆———

If you can't find an answer, look for a reason to believe.

INSPIRATION

Give yourself the best, you deserve it.

---

Have no fear of change. Loosing something good
could be making room for something great!

---

There has to come a point when you say to yourself
"I'm done being my own roadblock".

---

Decide your destination with your mind,
use your heart to get you there.

---

There is way too much to smile about
to submerge yourself in worry.

You're not going to win *all* of your battles,
but you will be happy knowing you fought.

---

If you are going to cheat, do so on your fears,
and commit to your dreams.

---

We all have gifts, don't allow fear
to keep you from opening yours.

---

You may have to squint to see it, but even in what seems
to be your darkest hour, there is always light.

---

Your only limitations are the ones that you acknowledge.

Happiness isn't about what surrounds you, but how you view it.

―――――◆―――――

Procrastination is a disease that attacks and kills potential.

―――――◆―――――

It's bad when we let others talk us out of our dreams,
but it's horribly worse when we do it to ourselves.

―――――◆―――――

We should be in a constant state of change.
If you are not changing you are not growing.

―――――◆―――――

Don't imitate others, learn from them
and be what you were born to be, *you!*

The perfect time to look to the past is in thanks
of what God brought you from.

---

Don't waste your time thinking about what you could have been
when what you could be is ahead of you.

---

The more you support the dream of others the closer you will be
to witnessing yours become a reality.

---

What you think is happening TO you could be happening FOR you.

---

Without struggle we would never experience
the magic that is... Hope.

There is no storm too big for God to calm.

―――――◆―――――

You don't have to concentrate on "not being like everyone else"
God already did it for you.

―――――◆―――――

Make this the day that you begin making opportunities
instead of waiting for them.

―――――◆―――――

We are always presently creating our future,
do good and watch good come to you.

―――――◆―――――

Change your mindset from "Whose going to let me?"
to "Whose going to stop me!"

# LIFE

*"For our present troubles are small and won't last very long. Yet they produce for us a glory that vastly outweighs them and will last forever."*

**2 Corinthians 4:17 KJV**

In everyone's lifetime there comes unforgettable moments. We never forget exactly what time the event happened and where we were when it did; and usually, that moment is etched into our memories forever, although it only lasted for a matter of seconds.

For me, those moments include the first time my father let go of the bike when teaching me how to ride, the first time I saw the children my grandparents had adopted, who were my age. Finally, I thought, I don't have to be lonely any more.

I will always remember the moment I walked across the stage of my high school graduation after failing time after time, signing an enlistment contract with the Army, the morning of September 11, stepping off the plane back in the U.S. after leaving combat in Iraq, a reflective moment during my second college graduation, and the first sight of my very own books in the freshly opened box. These moments and many others shaped my life in some way. A few even made it possible for me to pivot in another direction. But none had more of an effect on me than the moment I learned my youngest brother had passed.

His name is Andrew, and he saw only 18 years of life. I remember I was home early from work, but the sunlight seeping through the closed curtains was beginning to fade with the day. I was on my couch, trying to relax but unable to escape thoughts of my problems and circumstances. I cringed at the idea of continuing in a job I hated; my head and heart ached as I thought about my dead-end relationship; I was feeling harassed by non-stop calls from bill collectors; and I felt swamped and depressed by the assignments due for class. But in a moment, I would quickly come to realize how trivial those "problems" were.

My sister, who has always played the role of "bearer of bad news" in our family, called. Her first words were, "Have you heard from Dad yet?" Anytime she says something like that I know for sure something is amiss.

"No," I answered, "what's wrong?"

"Andrew went swimming and never came up. They are searching for him now, but they think he may have died out there."

Before I could even hang up the phone to call my father I was already clinging to denial.

When I asked my father what happened, I will never forget the words he uttered. They remain as fresh in my head as though they are being said as I write them. "Well, it looks like Andrew has drowned."

My heart immediately dropped to the floor; tears followed. Not knowing exactly how to handle the news, I paced back and forth, unable to imagine how horrifying those last seconds must have been for a person with whom I grew up and shared so many memories, whom I loved. At his funeral six days later, I stood over his body, this boy who had been very much alive just a week prior to that moment, and I thought, Wow, my little brother was blessed with so little life. How is it that we take life for granted?

It's a sad story, sure, but everyone has stories that evoke such pain. Fortunately, for most of us sadness and pain are but a portion of life. What is more sad is that, all too often, we wait too long to start living the lives that we were meant to live. Whether Andrew waited too long or not, he did leave gifts behind. My brother's passing brought our family closer together than we had been for as long as I can remember. Members of the family who had not spoken to one another in years as a result of arguments were reunited in friendship. And "I love you", once unspoken, now comes at the end of every conversation. Andrew's gift is a simple lesson, one we learn at every funeral yet seem to forget afterwards: Life is short, and as you read these words, not another minute is promised.

Overall, this book is about life. I have written it as a way to open myself up so that anyone can benefit from learning the lessons I have learned. I love my brother dearly, but I understand that his death was the culmination of a series of decisions that, inevitably, did not serve him well. He had fallen victim to his own temper, indulged in illegal drugs, befriended negative influences, and turned a deaf ear to lessons offered in words. Instead, he would have to receive them by the chastisement of life, which shows no favoritism among us. Unfortunately, we don't always get to learn from every lesson, especially if it is our last.

The love lost by the fault of our own hands doesn't always return, words uttered can never be retracted, and the best "I'm sorry" can do is make a scar out of a wound.

We are the result of our experiences, thoughts, and decisions, and the direction of our journey is mapped step by step, by each of them, great or small. Any one of those decisions may have an impact on the rest of our lives. It is ironic and astonishing that the difference between living for years to come and not seeing the rest of the day, or a family remaining divided or coming together in love and remembrance, rested upon a young boy's last decision: I will go to the lake today.

*"The tragedy of life is not that it ends so soon, but that we wait so long to begin it."*

**W. M. LEWIS**

For as long as I have considered the subject, I have been without a doubt that, put simply, life is about living. Not to be held down by headache and a heavy heart, or to slave for money and material things, or to be chained to anything that would keep us from smiling in retrospect when we take our last breath on Earth. Life is about being free. It's about enjoying every moment, and cherishing them all because of what they are—precious. Live, and live wisely.

In addition, we all have a purpose. After being pulled from deep waters, mere seconds away from drowning, walking away from a car accident in which the vehicle flipped several times, and listening to a bullet sing as it zipped by my ear during combat in Iraq, I refuse to believe that we were simply born to die. We all have a purpose—the obligation to live our lives to the fullest. There is a purpose for every life. There is too much creation for us to enjoy, and so many ways we can produce for the benefit of our brothers and sisters to believe otherwise. Make a commitment to yourself that from this day forward you will begin living the life that you deserve, a life that you can be proud of, and one that you can be happy about on the way out. Because you only get one, and you don't know—no one knows—when your ride is going to be over.

Finally, I close out the chapter with this: The two most important life decisions you will ever make are whom you choose to be by your side and whom you choose to live in your heart. When all is said and done, when you've gone through life and achieved it all, the person you chose to be by your side has been there for life, and whomever you chose to live in your heart, will be there with you for eternity.

Rest in Peace, Andrew. May the readers of this book forever carry your gift in their hearts.

## Life in Five Short Chapters

**CHAPTER 1**

I walk down the street.

There's a deep hole in the sidewalk.

And I fall in.

I am lost. I am helpless. It isn't my fault.

It takes forever to find a way out.

**CHAPTER 2**

I walk down the same street.

There is a deep hole in the sidewalk.

I pretend I don't see it. I fall in again.

I can't believe I am in the same place.

But it isn't my fault.

It takes a long time to get out.

**CHAPTER 3**

I walk down the same street and there is a deep hole
in the sidewalk.

I see it there, and still I fall in.

It's a habit.

But my eyes are open and I know where I am.

It is my fault and I get out immediately.

**CHAPTER 4**

I walk down the same street.

There is a deep hole in the sidewalk.

I walk around it.

**CHAPTER 5**

I walk down a different street.

*by Portia Nelson*

It's amazing how much more simple our lives would be if only we had the sense to skip chapters two, three, and four, or listen to the voices that warn us about the dangerous path in the first place.

When what is in you is stronger than what is being done to you,
you will always be victorious!

---

If your expectations for the worst are constant, you will treat
every situation as such, and you will never fail to find,
what you were looking for.

---

What sense does it make to fear dying AND living?

---

There are those that learn from others mistakes, those that learn
from their own, and those that never learn.

---

Keep your hands out of God's plans, that includes what
he is trying to do in your life.

People will appreciate what you give them, but they will hold on to, respect, and protect what you make them work for.

---

We can't regret everything, some mistakes are made to appreciate.

---

What is the point of truth always coming to light
if you are going to cover your eyes?

---

For every moment that we inhabit the earth without the Lord
in our hearts we gamble with our eternity.

---

For every minute you spend angry you lose
60 seconds of happiness.

Every person that walks into your journey isn't meant to stay,
and sometimes you have to let them go to march on.

Words tend to echo, may the ones that flow from your lips
bless the people they touch.

You never lose friends, you just find out who your real ones are.

There are too many new mistakes to make to be making
the same ones over and over again.

Life is too short to hold on to anger and grudges.
We all know it, but only think of it at funerals.

Most of the things that are making you sad
are things you are holding on to.

---

Be just as swift to extend your arms to give
as you would be to receive.

---

Taking ownership of your burdens will take you halfway
to lightening your load.

---

Be selective in your battles, sometimes peace
is better than being right.

---

Love someone who doesn't deserve it, but not to the extent
that it cripples your ability to love those that do.

You are a constant project, responsible
for your own construction or destruction.

---

If you are going to be over worked and under paid,
it should be a job you love doing.

---

The best promises to keep are the ones you make to yourself.

---

Sometimes it takes a storm to force that thing out
of your life that the wind just couldn't blow away.

---

You would be a fool not to be concerned about
the future, you have to live there.

You have to know where you are before you create
the path to where you want to be.

―――――◆―◆―◆―――――

People will show you over and over how much they don't care
about you, but how much could you possibly care
about yourself if you choose to ignore it?

―――――◆―◆―◆―――――

It's funny how God has all the answers and we all know it,
yet we go to him dead last for them.

―――――◆―◆―◆―――――

The worst deceptions are the ones we practice on ourselves.

―――――◆―◆―◆―――――

You can't always give as much as you'd like, sometimes you have
to give what a person can handle.

You will live in a state of trouble if you make denial your home.

————◆————

For every time you shovel up the past, it will be that
much more difficult to bury it again.

————◆————

Time fades even great friendships, we just have to be thankful
that their seasons had remarkable timing.

————◆————

You should live with an open heart, but you can't tell everyone
to make themselves at home.

————◆————

The fastest way to finding you is by seeking God.

Past pains will chain your present and future to misery
if you allow yourself to stay bound to them.

---

Faith will afford you the patience to keep your hands
out of God's plan.

---

Don't let an opportunity to let someone know you care pass.

---

Confidence is the most attractive thing a person can wear.

---

Sometimes the things you can't change end up changing you.
Just make sure it's for the better.

Be louder in your thanks for the good than you are
in complaining about the bad.

---

Sometimes we can't even trust ourselves, trust the one
that knows you better... God!

---

The first step in learning from your mistakes is accepting them.

---

Nothing lasts forever, but there is nothing wrong with fighting to
keep the things you love for a little bit longer.

---

You can't be honest with anyone about who you are
if you are lying to yourself.

You can't depend on your eyes when your mind is out of focus.

————◆—◆—◆————

Don't judge people by their past, be encouraged by their triumph.

————◆—◆—◆————

The ones worthy to be in your life are the ones that add to it.

————◆—◆—◆————

People will prove you right and wrong in the most unfortunate
of ways, believe what they show you.

————◆—◆—◆————

Sometimes moving forward means standing still.

Worrying only doubles the trouble.

---

Don't judge a person by their past, be inspired by their testimony and the fact that they made it through.

---

You have to make changes to see a change in your life.

---

One friend of action is worth more than a million talkers that call themselves a friend.

---

Don't wait until your problems grow roots to attack them, kill them while they are seeds.

People may do hurtful things because forgiveness is easier
to ask for than permission.

---

Trust people for what you KNOW them to be,
not what you THINK they should be.

---

Even if you could press fast forward, you'd still have
to go through it.

---

Love saying yes, but definitely know how to say NO.

---

Quitting is easy, it's living with it that's the hard part.

# INNER BEAUTY & SELF-LOVE

*"Do not let your adorning be external—the braiding of hair and the putting on of gold jewelry, or the clothing you wear—but let your adorning be the hidden person of the heart with the imperishable beauty of a gentle and quiet spirit, which in God's sight is very precious."*

**1 PETER 3:4**

Although many choose to ignore the presence, much less the relevance, of the two, there is no denying the sheer power and impact that inner beauty and the sense of self-love—or the absence of them—have on our everyday lives. They are intertwined and bound together. What we look like on the inside attracts people and even things to our lives and how we feel about ourselves determines what we allow to remain in our lives; both have the opportunity either to build us up or cause our ultimate destruction.

# INNER BEAUTY

Often we wonder why certain things—good and bad—have come into our lives. The Law of Attraction would say that what comes into our lives are things, people, situations, and opportunities that we ourselves have attracted. Most of us attempt, for at least a moment, to wrap our minds around an apparent targeting of bad luck—and great luck, too—in life and relationships, when many times the answer is within.

In order to attract, we must first project. Therefore, if we find that we attract the same types of partners, could we not perhaps attribute it to something we are projecting? What about the "good luck"? Is it not conceivable that exuding positivity could bring positive things into your life? Think about it in the difference between a smile and a glare; one is contagious, opening the possibility of making another's day with the simple gesture, and the other a dangerous type of infection, opening a door to anger and possible confrontation. If those two things can be the cause of such different reactions, imagine how many chances we have each day to project either positivity or negativity, and the difference our choices may be making in our lives, and in the lives of other people.

What we project is nothing more or less than a reflection of what we look like on the inside. It is, in fact, an accurate measure of our inner-beauty.

*"Even so every good tree bringeth forth good fruit; but a corrupt tree bringeth forth evil fruit."*

**MATTHEW 7:17**

The truth is, who we are on the inside is always projected by our actions, words, and energy, and the things that we attract in our lives are reflections and manifestations of the fruit that we have produced. Many are afraid to look within because they fear what we may, or may not, see; but as much as we may try to suppress it, what is in our heart will always find a way to show through our actions or words. Regardless of the effort we may place into hiding the ugliness within, that ugliness will always find a way to show itself, just as those who may want to conceal the good in them, out of fear of being hurt, can only hold it in for so long.

When I first gave my life to the Lord, I remember I was battling a problem with my tongue; I could not stop cursing. Before I'd decided to make the change, I had grown from a moderate curser to a full-blown professional. I thought I sounded cool and that I made my points more effectively, but people would often tell me that I didn't look right cursing. Its progression was only a testament to how ugly my heart was becoming.

Changing was an uphill climb. Anytime an obscenity would slip from my mouth it hurt me, because I knew that my words were my fruit, a manifestation of some of the uncleanliness that still stained my heart. With tearful eyes I would pray a simple prayer, "Lord please create in me a clean heart, so that my fruit will be good and pleasing in your eyes." My struggle was more than just the utterance of curse words; I was still producing ugliness, negativity, and things that would attract the unwarranted.

Having true inner beauty is the key to attracting into our lives things that we desire, such as good relationships, prosperity, and a sense of fulfillment. It begins with taking a look inside ourselves and conducting an honest self-assessment, and then cleaning house, so to speak. We spend so much time beautifying the external, which is not only temporal but often attracts undesirable attention, while we neglect the internal. As long as we neglect that part of us, we lose, but when we begin to work on and boost that inner-beauty, it radiates in everything we do, and in turn we attract the beautiful parts of life that we all deserve.

# SELF~LOVE

Most people would say that they have a healthy love for themselves without having a clear idea of what it means to love. Love is the simplest truth, yet the hardest thing to properly describe; in fact, everyone seems to have their own description, even though the Bible gave us the perfect one.

*"Husbands, love your wives, even as Christ also loved the church, and gave himself for it."*

**EPHESIANS 5:25**

The Bible tells us that to love is to be willing to die for what we love, but many of us don't even like ourselves enough to protect ourselves from harm. To simplify this point further, would you risk your life to save your parents? Would you be willing to fight for the honor of your best friend? With your answers in mind, ask yourself this: What hardship in your life are you allowing yourself to endure? It is all too common that we fight for the well-being of everyone except ourselves. We claim to love ourselves, yet we stay in bad relationships, we allow people to belittle and degrade us, and we put up with people giving us less than we deserve but just enough to keep us around. You see, the easiest way to gauge how much you really love yourself is by taking an honest look at your life and counting the unnecessary pains and burdens that you are refusing to cut out of your life, even while they are destroying it.

This is why self-love is so important. Take the issue of relationships for example. Most times when people are in toxic relationships and refuse to get out, it is because of a lack of self-love. I've proclaimed my self-love for as long as I can remember, but eventually that idea was really put to the test. I found myself in an abusive relationship. I had come to love a person so much that I allowed her to abuse me mentally, emotionally, verbally, even spiritually. This person was sucking the life out of me, until finally I had to be honest with myself. Not only did I love her more than me, but I was not loving myself at all. After all of this abuse, how could I honestly say that I had self-love? We don't allow our best friends to be so mistreated, but we allow ourselves to be? How much can a person love him- or herself if they are continuously subjecting themselves to lies, cheating, disrespect, and abuse? A person with true self-love doesn't stand for these things, rightfully, and neither should you!

We have to love ourselves enough to do what is best for us, even when it hurts—especially when it hurts . Here is a simple exercise: Look at yourself in the mirror, not as your reflection, but as a separate person, a best friend whom you love. Decide in that moment that you are going to protect that friend, as much as it is in your power, from all harm. Don't just say it, commit to it. Then give the person in the mirror the best you have to offer. That's love.

If you are going to be vain, be so about the way
you look on the inside.

---

All the cosmetics in the world can't disguise an ugly heart.

---

True self-love exists when you have learned to love the things
you dislike about yourself.

---

There is nothing more beautiful than a clean heart,
and all you have to do is ask God for it.

---

It's amazing how much a simple smile
can magnify a woman's beauty.

Appreciate the exterior, *love* what's on the inside.

---

You know its love when you can look in the mirror
and see God's Masterpiece.

---

Fall in love with [insert your name here]
and watch the world do the same.

---

If only we put half the effort into beautifying
our hearts as we do our faces.

---

Care less about a coke bottle frame or a V-shaped figure,
what's inside? That's what matters.

The most important thing you can carry is an attitude of gratitude.

---

It can't always be about how you feel,
think about what you deserve.

---

You don't have to go any further than a mirror to see a miracle.

---

One can tell how groomed they are internally
by the kind of people they attract.

---

You can't achieve self-gratification, self-love, or self-worth
if you're looking for it in everyone else.

The more self-love one has the less tolerance they have
for the things non-deserving of their time.

---

What you have to say about yourself matters more
than what others have to say about you.

---

We are all born beautiful, but many allowed to be made
ugly by their own actions and words.

---

Sometimes it's not the walking away that hurts so badly, but how
easy they made it look. You just have to remember for yourself,
the worth of what they are walking away from.

---

You deserve the absolute best, but you won't receive it
until you *know* this and act like it.

You attract what you project. Such a simple yet often over-looked truth.

# MOVING ON

*"Remember ye not the former things,*
*neither consider the things of old."*

**ISAIAH 43:18-19**

Moving on—from relationships or other circumstances in our lives—is one of the toughest things to do. The irony is that the things that are the hardest to move on from are typically the things that are holding us back. We become comfortable with, or addicted or attached to, people and things that keep us from fulfilling our own purpose, reaching our dreams, and achieving our goals.

We all hold on to the past, bad relationships, draining careers, and other burdens. Even when we see the pain and loss that we are causing, even when we see the beautiful future that awaits us, we remain stuck with a sturdy grip on heavy weights. We allow fear, ignorance, anger, and hurt to become a block of concrete around our feet. Regardless of what may be in front of us, we reject the idea that we can move on, and sometimes we deny that it's even necessary.

For years, I denied that being adopted had an effect on who I am, even as the inner void—which had formed when I had learned about it—slowly turned into a vacuum. Of course, I never gave much conscious thought to the adoption; I even prided myself on being able to push it to the back of my mind. But there is a difference between moving on from something and suppressing it. To move on from something, we must deal with it; I, however, ignored it. Unfortunately (or not, depending on how you look at it) we can ignore the symptoms of our inner issues for just so long. A few symptoms of my issue about my adoption was my inability to trust women despite my desire to have them around me, my need to always have a partner, and an apparent addiction to toxic relationships.

Needless to say, these symptoms were destructive not only to me, but to just about any kind of relationship I was in and to those who were involved. The destruction grew to a point where I had no choice but to deal with it. I forced myself to acknowledge the hurt and emptiness it had caused and the havoc I had allowed it to wreak. I considered what damage I would cause in my future if I refused to do something about it. Then I could rewrite the story of my adoption as a blessing. That is how I moved on so that I could start on a path of being a blessing for others and to myself. To move on—from any person, circumstance, or issue—is to gain freedom, but freedom, of course, is never free.

I am convinced that if we knew our expiration dates (in other words, how much time we have on Earth), moving on would not be so tough at all. If we could see the gifts that await us in our future, I'm sure we wouldn't hesitate. For example, would we stay with a partner who was not really right for us if we could see our soul-mate on the horizon? Would we hang on to grudges if we knew we were in our last hours? My guess, for both examples, is no, probably not.

One of my favorite stories of the Bible tells of the time when Jesus cursed the fig tree.

*"Now in the morning as he (Jesus) returned into the city, he hungered. And when he saw a fig tree in the way, he came to it, and found nothing thereon, but leaves only, and said unto it, Let no fruit grow on thee henceforward forever. And presently the fig tree withered away. And when the disciples saw it, they marveled, saying, How soon is the fig tree withered away!"*

**MATTHEW 21: 18-20 KJV**

The lesson is this: None of us has the time to invest energy into things that are not producing in our life, much less draining it. We all know there are things that we hold on to that it is in our best interests to let go.

Choose this moment to do so. Choose this moment to cut off anything that is not producing for you, that may be draining you of happiness or success, that is holding you back or holding you down. Just as Jesus showed in this scripture, do not hesitate. Deal with it, cut it off, and move on.

When you give your best to someone it is never good enough for,
that's the less you have to give the person it was meant for.

---

Don't allow yourself to catch a third degree burn
before you leave a "Hell" of a relationship.

---

When we think the biggest problem is that our significant
other doesn't care, it's really that we accept it.

---

Some are just fine with giving you just enough to keep you around,
as long as you are just fine with accepting it.

---

Let whatever you have been through be your fuel
to love just that much harder.

Stop renting your heart out, that's not fair
to the person it's meant for.

---

God can and WILL fix your heart, but you have
to give him ALL the pieces!

---

You can't fall for someone else when you are still trying
to pick yourself up from the last relationship.

---

If you can't love them enough to let them go,
love yourself enough to move on.

---

You made the mistake of letting me go, but it's really going to burn
when you see I've learned I can live without you.

You can only run to your friends complaining so much before you
look stupid running back to the same relationship.

---

You've got to be with someone that knows what
they have when they have you.

---

You can't change the past... but you can certainly let it go!

---

Just because destiny put you together doesn't mean
it was meant for forever.

---

Don't waste time allowing your break-up last longer
than the relationship.

If it's not adding to your life it's time to subtract it.

---

Don't be attached to how a person made you feel in the past.
The question is, "what have you been for me lately?"

---

Don't commit to someone committed to wasting your time.

---

God CAN and WILL mend your broken heart,
but you have to give him ALL of the pieces.

---

Don't hold on to someone whose needs you know you can't fulfill.
Chances are a third person will pick up the slack.

Why ignore a future that awaits to dwell on a past
that has long forgotten you?

---

The first step in letting go is in being honest with yourself
about the weight of what you are holding on to.

---

Don't hold on to something that is holding you from giving your
heart what it deserves.

# THE HOPE AND DESIRE
# FOR NEW LOVE

*"Many waters cannot quench love, neither can the floods*
*drown it: if a man would give all the substance of his*
*house for love, it would utterly be condemned."*

**SONG OF SOLOMON 8:7 KJV**

I t could be said that love, true love, is more sought after than anything else. Some would argue that money holds that position, or
fame, material things, external beauty, or success. But, in the event
that those things are gained, most would concede that without a
loved one to share it all with, all of those things mean next to noth-

ing. Our appetite for love is innate, and the moment we realize the type of love required to quench that thirst, the hope and desire for it is born. Of course, we look for it in different places, we set guidelines and restrictions on what it should look like, and we try to time its arrival. Yet still, while we are alone, we hope and dream of its arrival and that when it comes it's a perfect fit.

I began to dream of love as a very young boy. At thirteen, I was already on my knees highlighting prayers with requests for the perfect love. Every night, I prayed for God to bring someone into my life the next day, someone with whom I would grow together and grow old, and on that next day I would expect our paths to finally cross. It took a few years, but finally my eyes met those of the girl that I was sure He sent just for me. It was at a high school football game that I was not supposed to attend, on the side of the field where I was not supposed to be. Perfect! This had to be fate. Eye contact turned into brief conversation, the small talk turned into hours on the phone.

Eventually, growing feelings sent me to the payphone amidst the fury of a thunderstorm to ask her just one question: Will you be that love for me? And to that she happily answered, Yes. It's one of the favorite stories of my life. That relationship ended, and yet when it did, the hope for love was reborn.

A beautiful thing about life is how unexpectedly love finds us. I've bumped into it in a foreign country, under the strobe lights of a night club, in a seat just a few behind mine in class; it has even come as a result of a random search of friends on a social network. Still, there has never been more powerful love than the love I found in Christ, and the love that I found in myself.

An important thing to realize is that, even when you are single, you are in a relationship with yourself, and it's not until that relationship is perfected that you can be fully ready for a relationship with another person. Also, the quickest route to obtaining a great relationship with ourselves—as well as to finding the person meant for us—is by first fine-tuning our relationship with Christ.

*"But seek ye first the kingdom of God,*
*and his righteousness; and all these things*
*shall be added unto you."*

**MATTHEW 6:33 KJV**

The wait can be frustrating, the journey daunting, and experiences along the way can make us want to give up, but the hope for true love and a real relationship always remains. We should remember that, no matter what it seems like, your Creator loved you so much that He created someone solely for you. While you are wondering who that person is, her or she may be dreaming of the day when your hearts will meet. You may have convinced yourself that you are too broken for love, but there is someone who will prove to you that true love can heal the most shattered of hearts. Even if you think you are not good enough for love—that you don't deserve love—know that the moment that true love is revealed to you will be the moment you could live in for eternity.

Love made you and love freed you, so never think that it is not meant for you.

Until that real relationship "that true love" arrives, you have a responsibility to prepare yourself for it. In other words, making yourself easy to love and ready to love. Think of yourself as a house, and love the new resident. You may not know when that love is going to walk through the door, but when it does, you want make sure that your house is a place where love can feel at home. All the furniture is in place, the floors are clean, it has a freshness and warmth about it, and the décor is simply beautiful. Of course it may be far from perfect, but the one of the beautiful things about love is that it doesn't look for perfection; even more, what you may see as your flaws are the things that another will fall utterly in love with.

Believe that you are worth loving and that there is someone for you, feel free to hope while praying that God will guide that person into your life in His time, and prepare yourself to receive.

For as many times as your heart can be broken,
there is one that can make you believe in love again.

---

Focusing on the external rather than what is inside affords us
the ability to attract yet the inability to keep.

---

Don't allow your experiences with boys to ruin
your perception of men.

---

Don't let a person bring you down to a place where you
are unable to love anyone else.

---

Don't let falling hard for hard love harden your heart
towards your next love.

It can be a little tough truly learning to love yourself,
but if you won't go through the trouble, who else will?

———————◆◆◆———————

The true secret to attraction is in loving yourself.

———————◆◆◆———————

It would be a lot easier to pick a good partner
if people walked around inside out.

———————◆◆◆———————

If you are single, worrying is the first step in the wrong direction.

———————◆◆◆———————

Sometimes being single is the best cure.

Don't pass up a good man for a great dater.

———————◆———◆———————

You can trust your heart to lead only
when it is settled in the right place.

———————◆———◆———————

We were not made to be alone, but make sure your house
is in order before you let anyone in.

———————◆———◆———————

Single doesn't have to mean settle.

———————◆———◆———————

When your capacity to love is reduced,
so too is the ability for one to love you.

It takes too much time and energy to chase everything that catches
your eye, pursue what catches your heart.

---

Be yourself and you will attract a partner that is compatible
with YOU, not your image.

---

Worry less about finding someone to love,
and work toward becoming easier to love.

---

You can lure love in by making your inner-self
accommodating for it.

---

Someone will love you for who you are, but that doesn't mean
there isn't room to change for the better.

Even if you had a choice in who you fell for you'd still pick
the wrong person. Leave it to God.

Many will desire your heart, give it to the one that deserves it.

Being YOU is your best bet in finding someone
who will love you for you.

Save the best parts of you for the ONE that deserves it.

A best friend is the best thing you can ask for in a partner.

Don't change for someone to like you when there is someone
who will love you for YOU.

---

No, you are not perfect, but there is someone
who isn't perfect without you.

---

Whatever you dislike about yourself, know that one day
those are the things that someone will love.

---

Don't be afraid to start a new beginning because
the last ending was bad.

---

Love will catch you off guard in the most unlikely places.

There is someone who will see ALL of your flaws
and still think you are beyond amazing.

———◆———

Don't give your heart away. People take special care
of what they pay a good price for.

———◆———

You were given the gift of life, and you only get to do it once,
so make sure it's with the right person.

———◆———

Desire real love, be patient enough for the right love.

———◆———

Love gets a bad rap when people attach its name to the wrong things.

Do the right thing with the wrong person
and you'll get pain in return.

---

The faster the race to a relationship the quicker it will be over.

---

True love comes to those that have the courage to love even after
the blows of life gives them every reason not to.

---

# RELATIONSHIPS

Relationships can be quite difficult. There is no point in sugar-coating reality; that's just how it is.

Because television and movies bombard us with love stories that just about always end happily ever after, our initial ideas about relationships are usually romantic and unrealistic. Certainly my idea of relationships mirrored that concept, but I was lucky enough to witness the love that my parents have always shared for each other.

After many painful and unhappy experiences with love, I learned the hard way that relationships can be quite difficult. They can be difficult on the mind, the soul, and especially the heart. But, when you can make a good relationship work, it's well worth the effort.

The idea behind a relationship is simple, actually. It may be defined as two or more concepts, objects, or people connected to each other, or the state of being connected. Seems easy enough. Even finding someone compatible isn't too hard, compared to what's to come in dating and being together. No, the hard part is when two completely different individuals attempt to connect on the level wherein they are coming together as one. This is where selflessness comes into play, along with compromise, communication, understanding, learning one another, give and take, trust, and sacrifice—these are just some of the things that are necessary to keep a relationship alive and well, and they are required from both individuals. Many people take a lifetime to understand this; by the time they do, they realize that they may have already found—and lost—what they had searched for a long time ago.

That was the case for me. After a quick marriage and swift divorce, I spent years on the dating scene, enduring every kind of high and low, only to realize that I had walked away from everything I could ever want and need. That was when I learned that first, we must succeed in our relationship with ourselves. I will never forget the sight of her tear-stained face as I ended our relationship. I will also never forget the feeling that this was something I would someday deeply regret.

Relationships are projects, but today too many are left unfinished. When working on one gets tough, we abandon it and move on to another. We continue this cycle until we come to the understanding that the best part of a relationship comes after the hardest part. We watch in awe as elderly couples achieve fifty-plus years of being together, and envy the love we can see in the eyes younger couples whose relationships have also passed the test of time. We say to ourselves, "Now that's love." We want it, but without understanding that the glue holding those couples together is made of more than love. They have a bond created by walking through the fire and emerging from it together. By the time we have this revelation and decide to give a relationship our all, we walk into it bearing scars and experiences we picked up along the way, which makes the new one that much harder to build.

Whatever traits we desire in a partner and in our relationships, the most important thing is how a person makes you feel; and when you find someone who makes you feel the way you should feel, hold on to what you have. There will be times when your love will be tested and your relationship under attack. The irony of love is that even though it is the most powerful force known to us, it sometimes requires a fight to gain and keep; but when it's right, it's well worth the fight.

Actions speak louder than words but sometimes
your partner just needs to hear it.

———

The fastest way to lose a man is
to make him feel like he is less of one.

———

Don't get to down on yourself if your woman is never satisfied.
Eve had the world and the only man in it,
and it still wasn't enough.

———

Trust works to the benefit of your heart ONLY when
your mind is void of stubborn naiveté.

———

The problem with "space" in a relationship is,
there is always someone else willing to fill it.

Love is unconditional but patience has its limits.

---

If a man really wants something he will find a way,
if not, he will find excuses.

---

When actions show it, the words "I love you"
are only icing on the cake.

---

Assuming will consume your conscious and gnaw
on the framework of your relationship. Communicate.

---

One may never get caught, but there is always
a price to pay for cheating.

Don't take your partner for granted,
even the strongest feelings fade when ignored.

---

Don't be so quick to close the book,
the best chapter may be a page away.

---

The worst feeling is watching them work so hard in everything
but the relationship, but who's to blame if we allow it?

---

When they have the title but are not acting the part,
it's time for a demotion.

---

We wait for the bow after the rain, but walk away from
the impending love after the pain.

There is a very noticeable difference between knowing you matter
to someone and thinking you do.

———

One may deserve a second chance, but that shouldn't
give reason to waste the first one.

———

Arguing doesn't necessarily mean you're in a bad place,
dead silence however... does.

———

Small deeds done with great love go a long way.

———

Committing to a person's happiness when they are unsure
about they want will leave you in an uphill battle.

The more you make him feel like a wonder the less chance
he will wander to another woman.

––––––◆––––––

Every time you kiss your man do it as if you were
tip toeing to touch a star.

––––––◆––––––

It's the small, thoughtful, and unexpected that wins
and keeps a woman's heart.

––––––◆––––––

The length of your relationship will be based on how many times
the two of you can fall in love with the same person
over and over again.

––––––◆––––––

You have to give some of yourself to be with someone else.

Any man can take care of the bill. Be impressed
by how he handles your heart.

---

You know someone loves you when your happiness
is essential to their own.

---

Relationships are projects that we too often leave unfinished,
not realizing that sometimes the best part of the relationship
comes after the hardest.

---

The worst kind of loneliness is the kind
that exists in the relationship.

---

The most important trip you can make in your relationship
is meeting your partner halfway.

## Wear YES on Your Heart — J. L. FORD

You know its love when it looks completely ridiculous
to everyone else.

---

Part of staying in love is forgiving, and being grateful
that you have it.

---

A relationship is like an airplane, get on
with too much baggage and its going nowhere.

---

When a man truly loves a woman's smile...
he will do just about anything to see it.

---

If you can't forgive and forget you have
to at least forgive and... never bring it up again.

You don't need to know the definition of love
when your heart is experiencing it.

———◆—◇—◆———

Even when you "think" you are tired of loving,
your heart will keep you in a war.

———◆—◇—◆———

There's no fast forward to tell you if it's worth the wait,
just look at the reality and listen to your heart.

———◆—◇—◆———

It shouldn't take a person walking away
for their value to become clear.

———◆—◇—◆———

Strive to love like God & allow your partner
to teach you how to love them.

Love is blind but it shouldn't be invisible. There should be "Show&Tell" as much as possible in your relationships.

---

Good communication requires ACTION after the conversation.

---

You can't be impossible AND expect happiness.

---

Don't be the rebel that revolts against the ones that loves you.

---

The heart is the strongest muscle but when you are holding someone's else's, be mindful of how easily it tears when it cares.

Sometimes the change in your relationship starts
with the change in you.

---

Looking for better when you already have amazing
could leave you with NOTHING.

---

Sometimes you have to show a person that you can live without
them in your life for them to act like they deserve to be in it.

---

Love needs only one thing to grow, more love.

---

How can you expect a person to understand you if you
haven't taken the time to understand you first?

Don't be more than a friend but less than a lover,
it's either one or the other.

---

You attract people by what you display, you keep them
by what you posses.

---

Simply put, your relationship should be making you a better person.

---

Relationships are full of games, but don't be surprised when one
person leaves because they are tired of playing.

---

Love fearlessly.

Don't be a knife; giving praise should come just
as easily as handing out criticism.

---

Listening is hollow without understanding.

---

Even if you know what you have, don't act like you can never lose it.

---

It's not always the man's fault. There are women with GOOD men,
but have not the slightest idea.

---

You won't have to beg for a commitment from one
that really wants to be with you.

If you are the only one trying, the life of the "relationship" will
depend on how long you can carry the burden alone.

---

The happiness in a relationship should be on-going,
and not just a memory.

---

The saying goes "don't change who you are for anyone"
but if it's for the better, perhaps you should consider it.

---

Don't deny expressing your feelings to "keep the peace",
a person that wants to be with you will communicate with you.

---

6 billion people in the world, a man makes a woman feel like she
is the only one, and a real woman appreciates it.

You can break yourself trying to fix someone else.
Some things you have to let go and leave to God.

---

If a man hits you, he may not ever do it again,
but YOU don't stick around to find out.

---

Don't thirst for love so bad that you create
an illusion of it from its complete opposite.

---

Don't let the day you wake up realizing how perfect your partner
is be the day that person wakes up with the one who already knows.

---

Be careful not to fall in love with unlovable people,
you may adopt their traits.

Sometimes the best jump start to a dying relationship is... the truth.

Even if you can't handle the truth you deserve it.

Sometimes the answer is as simple as... He faked the whole thing.

You may be able to make a man lust for you,
but you can never make a man love you.

Some live in a dream of what they just know their relationship
could be while precious time is passing in reality.

If there were such a thing as a perfect partner or relationship
there would be no room for God.

---

The simple ingredient for a successful relationship is TWO people
with the desire to make it work.

---

Love doesn't mean that a person is going to wait around
for you to love them back, and nor should it.

---

Sometimes single means "working on a relationship with myself".

---

Wanting someone that doesn't want you will
unnecessarily tear your heart in two.

Love itself is always right, its people that do it wrong.

———◆◇◆———

Both men AND women do a lot better when they realize there
is more to a woman that her figure.

———◆◇◆———

The ones that make it work learned that the best part
of a relationship comes after the hardest part.

———◆◇◆———

"I'm a lover not a fighter" is an oxymoron.
True love often requires the greatest fight.

# HUMOR

*"And Sarah said, God hath made me to laugh, so that all that hear will laugh with me."*

**GENESIS 21:6 KJV**

Life is definitely nothing short of a roller coaster ride. With its ups and downs, its twists and turns, it's no surprise that sometimes we lose sight of the fact that every second of this ride is meant to be treasured, appreciated, enjoyed, and of course, not taken too seriously. Even on those unexpected dips where all may seem lost, as long as we have life we have the means to offer ourselves the simple joy and medicine of laughing at it.

## Wear YES on Your Heart — J. L. FORD

One of the things I have always admired most about my father is his ability to find something to laugh about, even in the worst situations; and when laugher is not an option, he is always good for a smile. I recall a time when we had so little that we had to search through our furniture to find enough money to buy spaghetti for dinner. Instead of letting the idea of being poor ever get us down, my little sister and I took after our father and made fun of the situation, finding a reason to laugh with every penny we managed to dig up.

I have many stories to illustrate my point. I laughed while tears of fear rolled down my cheeks as an elderly woman held my hand on my first flight; I stood in the middle of a store and chuckled at the $3.83 that I had left to my name, trying to think of how I was going to buy enough groceries to make it through the week. I laughed when I received notice that I was going back to Iraq for a second tour of combat, and though it was in disbelief, I even mustered a smile when I received the news that that the military was holding me beyond my separation date to keep me at war. When my brother passed, only a year before the publication of this book, I stepped to the podium at his funeral to offer some words of encouragement—and laughter, too, because even in the midst of death, memories give us reason to laugh at life.

Laughing at life is easier said than done, especially in the worst of circumstances, but it becomes easier as we begin to again understand that life is meant to be enjoyed. I say again because as children we understood that. We went about our daily routine of making the world our playground without a care in it, and we laughed at everything. When we found trouble, we laughed and when things got tough we found something to smile about, revitalizing our joy. The only difference between now and then is that somewhere along the way we started taking life seriously.

*"Rejoice evermore. Pray without ceasing. In every thing give thanks: for this is the will of God in Christ Jesus concerning you."*

**1 THESSALONIANS 5:16-18 KJV**

Laughter is a gift, a reliever of stress, pain, and the day-to-day conflicts and hardships that we endure. Even more, the benefits of a good laugh are infectious—the beautiful kind of infectious, that is. One good laugh produces the domino effect, touching everyone nearby, just as a simple smile warms the heart of whoever sees it.

Life is no joke, but it is full of laughing matters. Whenever you find a reason, have a good laugh, and when life knocks the wind out of you, catch your breath, laugh in its face, and hit back even harder.

The best way to remember your girl's birthday is
to forget it one time.

―――――◈―◇―◈―――――

There is no use in lying. I've never met a woman that didn't have a
better memory than me.

―――――◈―◇―◈―――――

There are a lot of great bargain shoppers that pick the wrong men.

―――――◈―◇―◈―――――

Passion is a powerful spring void of rationale, reason, and direction.
But at least it feels good.

―――――◈―◇―◈―――――

Forgive and remember, just don't keep bringing it up.

The key to listening to a woman is to hear what she is not saying...
but honestly, I'd rather they just talk

---

You know you've been at it a while when your partner is the one
you spend the shortest time on the phone with.

---

If someone asks why you are still single,
tell them you were born that way.

---

It's not always nagging; they just want you to be what you sold them
in the beginning. But sometimes... It's just nagging.

---

By trade, **J.L.FORD** is a writer, motivational speaker, and author consultant. At heart he is an incurable optimistic who believes the best is in store for those that believe in themselves. J.L. is originally from Webster, Florida. He is a two-time combat veteran currently working towards a Ph.D. in Sociology.

CPSIA information can be obtained at www.ICGtesting.com
Printed in the USA
LVOW042032201211

260341LV00001B/400/P